"EMPOWERING WOMEN TO LEAD, SECURE, AND BREAK BARRIERS IN TECH AND CYBERSECURITY."

YOU ARE NO LONGER WAITING FOR PERMISSION.
YOU ARE BUILDING NEW FUTURES. KEEP RISING. KEEP BREAKING THE CODE."
— DR. CHERYL COOPER

BY
DR. CHERYL COOPER
CYBERSECURITY LEADER | AUTHOR | ADVOCATE FOR WOMEN IN TECH

About Author

Dr. Cheryl Cooper is an award-winning cybersecurity leader, author, and speaker with over 15 years of experience in Governance, Risk, and Compliance (GRC). As a U.S. Navy Veteran and Doctor of Computer Science, she has built her career on breaking barriers and building bridges for women — especially Black women and women of color — to thrive in the male-dominated world of tech and cybersecurity.

From boardrooms to classrooms, Dr. Cooper is known for her visionary leadership and unapologetic advocacy for equity, inclusion, and empowerment. She currently serves as the President of the Women in CyberSecurity (WiCyS) Kansas City Chapter and has worked with Fortune 100 companies to lead cybersecurity strategy and digital risk initiatives that protect critical infrastructure.

Her books — Hood to Hooded: A Black Woman's Choice to Rise and Breaking the Code: Winning Strategies for Women in Cybersecurity and Tech — have inspired thousands to reclaim their voices, own their brilliance, and rewrite their future.

Dr. Cheryl Cooper

Cybersecurity Leader| Global Keynote Speaker| President Women in CyberSecurity (WiCyS) Kansas City | Skilled in Cyber Resilience Strategy & GRC | Consultant| Author Hood to Hooded| Author of Breaking the Code

Follow and Connect with Dr. Cooper:
🌐 drcherylcooper.com
LinkedIn:linkedin.com/in/drcherylcooper
Instagram: @drcherylcooper
Email: hello@drcherylcooper.com

Dr. Cooper created the Breaking the Code™ framework to help women confidently step into leadership, demystify GRC, and build meaningful, financially rewarding careers in cybersecurity. She is on a mission to make sure the future of tech looks like all of us — bold, brilliant, and beautifully diverse.

Table of Contents

Part 1: Personal Development & Building Leadership

Part 2: Starting a Career in GRC & Cybersecurity

Part 3: Networking, Interviewing & Promotion Prep

Part 4: What's Next - 12-Month Reflection & Monthly Affirmations

✨ Welcome to Your Leadership Journey

Congratulations on taking the next powerful step toward shaping your future in cybersecurity and GRC leadership.
This journal is not just a workbook—it's your personal leadership accelerator.

- You have the skills.
- You have the ambition.
- Now, it's time to claim your leadership

📘 Introduction: How to Use This Guided Journal

Welcome to Breaking the Code: Guided Journal & Workbook—your personal roadmap for mastering Governance, Risk & Compliance (GRC) and cybersecurity. This journal is structured into four distinct parts, allowing you to focus on the area's most relevant to your current stage in the journey:

Part 1: Personal Development & Building Leadership

- Develop the confidence and mindset to lead, even in male-dominated spaces.
- Reflect on your leadership style, challenge limiting beliefs, and craft action plans to overcome barriers.
- Learn from role-model exercises and interactive scenarios that prepare you for real-world leadership moments.

Part 2: Starting a Career in GRC & Cybersecurity

- Explore the fundamentals of GRC and cybersecurity.
- Discover your motivations, strengths, and career goals through self-discovery prompts.
- Follow bite-sized checklists to build essential skills, certifications, and community connections.

Part 3: Networking, Interviewing & Promotion Prep

- Prepare for interviews with customizable question-and-answer worksheets and elevator-pitch templates.
- Track your achievements and build a brag sheet to advocate for promotions and raises.
- Design a mini-Networking Strategy Plan and maintain a Contacts Tracker to grow your professional circle.

Part 4: What's Next – 12-Month Reflection & Monthly Affirmations

- Record your wins, lessons learned, and celebrations each month on dedicated reflection pages.
- Use the undated spreads to start at any point in your journey and track progress over twelve months.
- Finish with a Year-in-Review summary and a special Congratulations page to honor your growth.

Tips for Getting the Most from Your Journal

- Go at your own pace. There is no required order: jump to the section that best fits your current goals.
- Complete each section fully. All prompts, checklists, and exercises for a given theme live together, no need to flip back and forth.
- Reflect and revisit. Return to earlier parts whenever you need a refresher or new inspiration.
- Celebrate each step. Use Part 4 to honor your achievements and fuel the next chapter of your journey.

You hold the pen, let this journal guide you, support you, and remind you that every choice you make is one step closer to breaking the code in your career. Happy journaling!

🚀 PART 2 of 8

✨ Section 1B:

🔎 The Art of Self-Reflection

Reflecting on my career, I am reminded of the countless crossroads and decisions that have shaped my journey. Each choice, whether deliberate or serendipitous, has contributed to the path I walk today. Throughout my years mentoring aspiring cybersecurity professionals—particularly women and minorities—I've seen firsthand how hard it can be to recognize and embrace your unique strengths and potential.

It's time to cut out the noise. It's time to let your values and your ambitions guide your path.

✍️ Self-Reflection Survey

Rate yourself from 1 to 5 (1 = Strongly Disagree, 5 = Strongly Agree):

___ I am passionate about technology and enjoy keeping up with tech trends.
___ I find satisfaction in solving complex problems.
___ I can explain technical concepts to non-technical people effectively.
___ I work well under pressure.
___ I enjoy collaborating with others.
___ I am comfortable taking calculated risks.
___ I prioritize integrity in my work.
___ I am adaptable to change.
___ I enjoy taking leadership roles.
___ I am detail-oriented.
___ I am curious and like "tinkering."
___ I value continuous learning.
___ I think strategically.
___ I am comfortable with ambiguity.
___ I am resilient after setbacks.

📖 Reflection:

Where did you score highest?

Where did you score lower?

Were there any surprises?

🔎 Cybersecurity Career Compass

Rate yourself from 1 to 5 again (1 = Strongly Disagree, 5 = Strongly Agree):

___ I enjoy analyzing data.
___ I like ethical hacking.
___ I'm fascinated by security systems.
___ I thrive under pressure.
___ I enjoy explaining security strategy.
___ I want to develop security policies.
___ I enjoy investigating incidents.
___ I like encryption.
___ I follow cybersecurity news.
___ I am interested in cloud security.
___ I enjoy securing applications.
___ I'm excited about AI and IoT.
___ I like managing big projects.
___ I'm interested in risk management.

✍ Interpretation Guide:

- High scores on 1 and 9: Security Analyst or Threat Intelligence Analyst
- High on 2 and 3: Penetration Tester or Security Engineer
- High on 4 and 7: Incident Response or Digital Forensics
- High on 5 and 6: Security Consultant or CISO
- High on 8: Cryptography
- High on 10 and 11: Cloud or Application Security
- High on 12: Emerging Tech Security (AI/IoT)
- High on 13: Project Manager
- High on 14: GRC Specialist

🛡 Cultural Background Reflection

How has your cultural background influenced your problem-solving?

What cultural strengths do you bring to cybersecurity?

Have you faced stereotypes or cultural barriers? How did you overcome them?

✍ Personal SWOT Analysis

📌 Strengths:

What technical skills do I excel in?

……

What soft skills set me apart?

……

📌 Weaknesses:

What areas do I need to improve?

……

What feedback have I received?

……

📌 Opportunities:

What emerging trends align with my interests?

……

What gaps could my unique background fill?

……

📌 Threats:

What challenges might impact my career?

……

What biases must I overcome?

……

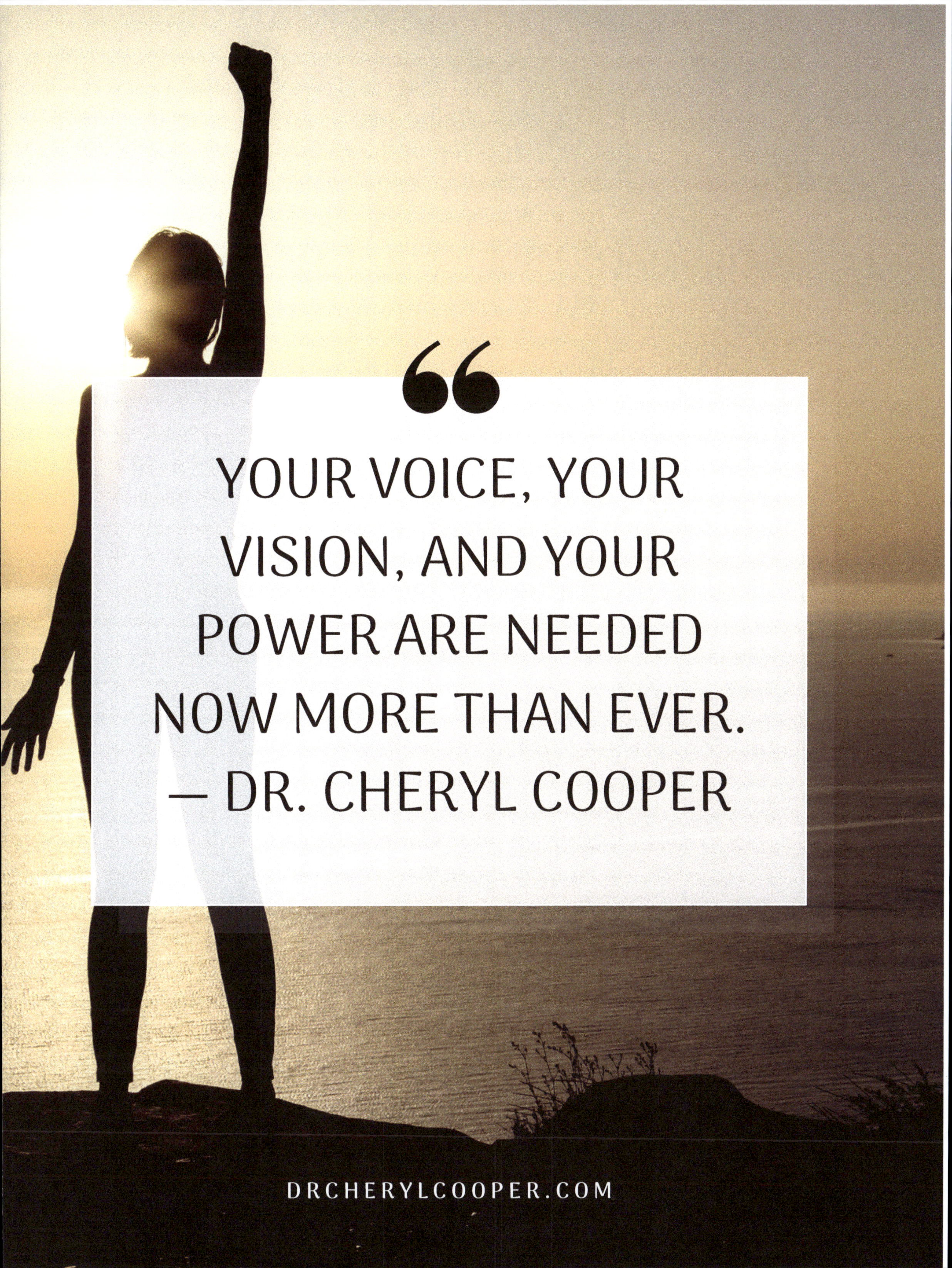
YOUR VOICE, YOUR
VISION, AND YOUR
POWER ARE NEEDED
NOW MORE THAN EVER.
— DR. CHERYL COOPER
DRCHERYLCOOPER.COM

🛡 Special Focus: Breaking Internal Barriers and Building Leadership Power

📚 Concept Summary:

Leadership barriers are real — but not unbreakable.
Especially for women of color, overcoming invisibility, bias, and imposter syndrome is part of the journey.

You are not an imposter.
You are an innovator.

🔎 Reflection Prompts:

When have I felt invisible at work or school?

How has bias or systemic barriers shaped my experience?

Where am I ready to show up unapologetically?

✨ Soft Skills Self-Assessment Exercise:

(Rate yourself 1–5 and reflect.)

Skill	Self-Rating	Reflection
Problem Solving		
Communication		
Critical Thinking		
Emotional Intelligence		
Collaboration		

🔥 Mentorship and Self-Advocacy Plan:

Identify one mentor or sponsor you want to connect with:

Identify one leadership opportunity you will advocate for:

📈 Success Tracker:

Week	Barrier Broken or Advocacy Action	Reflection

✅ END OF PART 5

🚀 PART 5 of 8

✨ Section 2:

Building Leadership Confidence

📚 **Concept Summary:**

Confidence isn't about never doubting yourself.
It's about **moving forward despite doubt** — and acting from a place of power.

Today, we build the type of confidence that **can't be shaken** by bias, fear, or setbacks.

🔎 Reflection Prompts:

When have I successfully led, even without an official title?

What strengths do I underestimate in myself?

How would I show up if I fully trusted my voice and leadership?

✨ Self-Leadership Affirmations Exercise:

Create 3–5 affirmations you can recite daily:

I am ______________________________

I lead with __________________________

My voice ___________________________

I create ____________________________

I deserve ___________________________

🔥 Apply It Challenge:

Take one bold visibility action this week:

Speak in a meeting
Post on LinkedIn
Volunteer to lead a small project

📈 Success Tracker:

Week	Confidence Action Taken	Reflection

✨ Empowerment Quote:

"Success is liking yourself, liking what you do, and liking how you do it."
— Maya Angelou

🚀 PART 3 of 8

🛡️ Special Focus: Power Moves for Thriving in Male-Dominated Industries

Building Visibility, Confidence, and Influence

📚 Introduction

You are not here to blend in. You are here to lead.
In male-dominated industries, it's easy for women — especially women of color — to be overlooked, underestimated, or excluded.
But your voice, your presence, and your leadership are essential to the future of cybersecurity and GRC.
Let's claim the space that belongs to you.

"Power is not given to you. You have to take it."
— Beyoncé

🔎 Reflection Prompt:

Recall a time you felt invisible or underestimated at work. How did it affect you?

How would you show up differently now?

📚 Presence Protocol Action Plan

📌 Physical & Strategic Presence Strategies:

Strategic Seating: Choose visible, central positions.
Body Language: Open posture, strong eye contact.
Purposeful Movement: Controlled, deliberate gestures.
Arrive early to meetings to claim space

📌 Vocal Presence Strategies:

Broken Record Technique: Calmly reclaim the floor if interrupted: "I'd like to finish my point."
Amplification Strategy: Align with allies who reinforce your contributions.
Speak up early and assertively in meetings.

📌 Follow-Up Strategies:

Send meeting summaries highlighting your contributions.
Document wins and decisions you influenced.
Stay visible between meetings with updates and progress reports

🔥 Confidence Builder Challenge

For the next 3 meetings:

Use the Broken Record Technique if interrupted.
Sit visibly and contribute early.
Follow up with a written summary of your input.

📖 Journal Reflection:

How did implementing these changes feel?

What reactions or shifts did you notice?

📚 Visibility Portfolio Starter Kit

✅ Start Your Visibility Tracker:

Achievement	Impact	Witness/Testimonial

✅ Tips:

Track leadership wins and project contributions monthly.
Collect short written feedback from mentors, peers, or leaders.
Document your leadership influence in quantifiable ways.

🛡 Power Move Challenge

Choose one Power Move to start immediately:

Implement the Presence Protocol
Build your Visibility Portfolio
Begin your Confidence Peak Performance Routine

✅ Find an accountability partner to check-in weekly.

✨ Affirmations for Thriving in Male-Dominated Spaces:

"I do not shrink to fit spaces. I expand them."
"I bring undeniable value to every table I sit at."
"My leadership is not optional. It is essential."

📖 Power Moves Final Reflection:

Which Power Move did you select?

What personal or professional growth did you notice?

✅ END OF PART 4

🚀 PART 3 of 8
🛡️ Special Focus:

Decrypting the Colorism Firewall

Building Power in the Face of Bias

📚 Introduction

In cybersecurity, firewalls are designed to block threats.
In society, however, women—particularly Black women and women of color—are often treated as the threat.
Colorism—discrimination based on skin tone—continues to taint professional spaces, impacting hiring, promotion, and leadership opportunities in the tech and cybersecurity industries.
We must recognize it. We must rise above it.
You are not here by accident. You are here by design.

" I will not shrink for a world too small to hold my brilliance."
— Dr. Cheryl Cooper

🔎 Understanding Colorism:

- **Definition:** Discrimination based on skin tone, even within the same racial or ethnic group.
- **Impact:** Widened wage gaps, leadership bias, hiring discrimination.
- **Reality:** Darker-skinned individuals face slower promotions, lower pay, and less visibility—even today.

✍ Reflection Prompts:

Have I experienced colorism, racism, or gender bias in my cybersecurity journey?

How has it impacted my career or personal confidence?

How has it impacted my career or personal confidence?

🛡 Action Plan: Managing Bias

Situation	Healthy Response	Empowerment Action
Encountering bias	Stay composed. Acknowledge internally but do not internalize.	Speak up when safe. Document incidents. Seek allies.
Being excluded or overlooked	Focus on demonstrating undeniable value.	Advocate for inclusion. Build your own tables if necessary.
Facing microaggressions	Respond calmly if appropriate. Document patterns.	Build resilience through community, mentorship, and visibility.

✨ Affirmations for Resilience:

Have I experienced colorism, racism, or gender bias in my cybersecurity journey?Bias cannot define my brilliance."

- "I am worthy of every opportunity I pursue."
- "My presence is powerful. My contributions matter."
- "Leadership flows through me, not around me."

📖 Closing Reflection:

What are 3 empowerment strategies I will use the next time I encounter bias?

🚀 PART 6 of 8

📚 Section 3:

Making Strategic Impact in GRC

📖 Concept Summary:

Strategic influence is how real leaders drive change in cybersecurity and GRC.
Today, you step beyond technical tasks into big-picture leadership thinking.

Your ideas matter.
Your strategies can transform organizations.

🔎 Reflection Prompts:

When have I successfully connected technical risks to business outcomes?

What leadership ideas do I want to propose to my team, department, or organization?

✍️ Strategic Leadership Initiative Draft Exercise:

Identify one risk, policy, or opportunity you want to address:

Draft a simple 1-page leadership initiative:
- Problem: ________________________________
- Strategic Solution: ___________________________
- Business Impact: _____________________________
- Next Steps: _________________________________

🔥 Apply It Challenge:

Share your leadership idea with a mentor, trusted peer, or decision-maker.

📈 Success Tracker:

Week	Barrier Broken or Advocacy Action	Reflection
Problem Solving		

✨ Empowerment Quote:

"Presence is not about volume. It's about unwavering conviction."
— drcherylcooper

📚 Section 4: Steering Beyond Barriers

📖 Concept Summary:

Leadership isn't about blending in — it's about steering the ship forward.
It's about bringing others along while building your own future.

You don't need permission to lead.
You only need clarity and courage.

🔎 Reflection Prompts:

How have I already broken barriers in my career or personal life?

How can I lift others as I rise?

✍️ Cyber Sisterhood and Allyship Map

Exercise:

List 5 allies, mentors, or sponsors you can lean on or support:

Ally / Mentor / Sponsor	How They Support You	How You Support Them

🔥 Apply It Challenge:

Amplify another woman's work, leadership, or voice publicly this month.

📈 Success Tracker:

Week	Barrier Broken or Advocacy Action	Reflection
Problem Solving		

✅ END OF PART 6

📜 Empowerment Affirmations Wall

✨ Cut out or post these affirmations where you will see them daily!

Affirmation
Own the Room
Speak Up Anyway
Confidence is a Practice, Not a Feeling
I Am Unstoppable
My Voice Creates Change
Brilliance Over Bias
Leadership is My Birthright

🔎 Section 1:

Gaining Clarity in GRC and Career Vision

Concept Summary:

Clarity is the foundation of all successful leadership. Without a clear vision, it's easy to drift or stall.
Today, we focus on defining your vision for a leadership career in cybersecurity and GRC.

✍️ Reflection Prompts:

What drew me to cybersecurity and GRC initially?

Where do I see myself in 3, 5, and 10 years in this field?

What unique value do I bring to cybersecurity leadership?

What challenges am I excited to solve?

What is GRC?"

Visibility isn't vanity– it's vitality.

Dr. Cheryl Cooper

GRC STANDS FOR GOVERNANCE, RISK, AND COMPLIANCE—A COMPREHENSIVE FRAMEWORK THAT ORGANIZATIONS EMPLOY TO ALIGN THEIR OPERATIONS WITH BUSINESS OBJECTIVES, MANAGE UNCERTAINTIES, AND ADHERE TO REGULATORY REQUIREMENTS.

GOVERNANCE

GOVERNANCE INVOLVES THE ESTABLISHMENT OF POLICIES, PROCEDURES, AND DECISION-MAKING PROCESSES THAT GUIDE AN ORGANIZATION'S DIRECTION AND ENSURE ACCOUNTABILITY. IT SETS THE FOUNDATION FOR ETHICAL CONDUCT AND STRATEGIC ALIGNMENT ACROSS ALL LEVELS OF THE ORGANIZATION.

RISK MANAGEMENT

RISK MANAGEMENT IS THE PROACTIVE IDENTIFICATION, ASSESSMENT, AND MITIGATION OF POTENTIAL THREATS THAT COULD IMPEDE AN ORGANIZATION'S ABILITY TO ACHIEVE ITS GOALS. BY ANTICIPATING RISKS, ORGANIZATIONS CAN DEVELOP STRATEGIES TO MINIMIZE THEIR IMPACT AND ENSURE RESILIENCE.

RISK MANAGEMENT

COMPLIANCE ENSURES THAT AN ORGANIZATION ADHERES TO LAWS, REGULATIONS, STANDARDS, AND INTERNAL POLICIES. IT INVOLVES IMPLEMENTING CONTROLS AND MONITORING MECHANISMS TO PREVENT VIOLATIONS AND PROMOTE A CULTURE OF INTEGRITY AND TRANSPARENCY.

TOGETHER, THESE COMPONENTS FORM AN INTEGRATED APPROACH THAT ENABLES ORGANIZATIONS TO OPERATE EFFECTIVELY, MAKE INFORMED DECISIONS, AND MAINTAIN TRUST WITH STAKEHOLDERS.

Career Progression Overview

1. Entry-Level Roles

Common Titles:
- GRC Analyst
- Compliance Associate
- Risk & Compliance Coordinator
- IT Auditor

Certifications:
- CompTIA Security+
- Certified in Cybersecurity (CC) by ISC²
- GRC Professional (GRCP) by OCEG

Essential Skills:
- Understanding of basic compliance frameworks (e.g., NIST, ISO 27001)
- Strong communication and documentation abilities
- Analytical thinking and attention to detail
- Familiarity with risk assessment methodologies

2. Mid-Level Roles

Common Titles:
- Risk Manager
- Compliance Manager
- IT Risk & Compliance Lead
- Internal Auditor

Certifications:
- Certified Information Systems Auditor (CISA)
- Certified in Risk and Information Systems Control (CRISC)
- Certified Governance, Risk and Compliance Professional (CGRC) by ISC²

Essential Skills:
- Proficiency in implementing and managing compliance programs
- Ability to conduct risk assessments and audits
- Knowledge of regulatory requirements (e.g., SOX, GDPR)
- Leadership and project management capabilities

Career Progression Overview

3. Senior-Level Roles

Common Titles:

- GRC Director
- Chief Compliance Officer (CCO)
- Chief Risk Officer (CRO)
- Chief Information Security Officer (CISO)

Certifications:

- Certified Information Securit Manager (CISM)
- Certified Information System Security Professional (CISSP)
- Certified in the Governance o Enterprise IT (CGEIT)

Essential Skills:

- Strategic planning and policy development
- Executive leadership and stakeholder communication
- Enterprise risk management
- Oversight of compliance and audit functions

Interactive Prompts

1. My Current Position:

Role Title: ______________________________

Years of Experience: ______________________________

Current Certifications: ______________________________

Key Skills: ______________________________

2. My Next Target Role:

Desired Position: ______________________________

Required Certifications______________________________

Skills to Develop: ______________________________

Target Timeline: ______________________________

Career Progression Overview

Short-Term Goals (Next 6 Months):

Long-Term Goals (Next 1–2 Years):

Note: This roadmap is a general guide. Individual career paths may vary based on organizational structures, industry sectors, and personal aspirations.

📦 Your GRC Essentials Kit

Checklist of Tools and Frameworks:

- NIST Cybersecurity Framework (CSF): Guidelines for improving cybersecurity risk management.
- ISO/IEC 27001: Standards for information security management systems.
- COBIT: Framework for developing, implementing, monitoring, and improving IT governance and management practices.
- Risk Registers: Tools for documenting and tracking identified risks.
- Compliance Dashboards: Visual tools for monitoring compliance status across various regulations.
- GRC Platforms (e.g., ServiceNow, RSA Archer): Integrated solutions for managing governance, risk, and compliance activities.

✍️ Interactive Prompt:

Tools I'm Familiar With:

Tools to Learn:

📈 Skills Development Planner

Here's the content for the Skills Development Planner page, designed to help users assess and plan their growth in both technical and non-technical areas within Governance, Risk, and Compliance (GRC) and cybersecurity.

Purpose:

This planner assists you in evaluating your current competencies, setting development goals, identifying resources, and tracking progress in key skill areas essential for success in GRC and cybersecurity roles.

🛠️ Skill Assessment Table

Skill Area	Current Level (1-5)	Goal Level (1-5)	Resources to Learn	Progress Notes
Risk Assessment			e.g., NIST SP 800-30, ISO 31000	
Compliance Frameworks			e.g., ISO 27001, HIPAA, GDPR	
Audit & Assurance			e.g., ISACA CISA training	
Policy Development			e.g., SANS Policy Templates	
Technical Writing			e.g., Technical Writing Courses	
Communication Skills			e.g., Public Speaking Workshops	
Project Management			e.g., PMP Certification, Agile Training	
Data Analysis			e.g., Excel, SQL, Data Visualization Tools	
Leadership & Management			e.g., Leadership Seminars, Mentorship Programs	
Cybersecurity Principles			e.g., CompTIA Security+, CISSP Training	

- Current Level: Rate your current proficiency on a scale of 1 (Novice) to 5 (Expert).
- Goal Level: Set your desired proficiency level.
- Resources to Learn: List courses, certifications, books, or mentors that can aid your development.
- Progress Notes: Document your journey, challenges faced, and milestones achieved.

✍️ Reflection Prompts

Top 3 Skills to Develop:

Action Plan for Each Skill:

Skill: ____
Steps to Improve: ____________________________________
Timeline: ____
Support Needed: ______________________________________

Potential Challenges and Solutions:

Challenge: ____
Solution: ____

Note: Regularly revisit this planner to update your progress and adjust your goals as needed. Continuous learning and adaptability are key in the ever-evolving fields of GRC and cybersecurity.

📚 Bibliography & Reference Guide

Frameworks & Standards

NIST Cybersecurity Framework (CSF) 2.0
National Institute of Standards and Technology (NIST). (2024). The NIST Cybersecurity Framework (CSF) 2.0. **PDF**

ISO/IEC 27001:2022 – Information Security Management Systems
International Organization for Standardization (ISO). (2022). ISO/IEC 27001:2022. **ISO Standard**

COBIT – Control Objectives for Information and Related Technologies
ISACA. COBIT Framework. **ISACA Resource**

GRC Tools & Concepts

Risk Register: How to Build One + Examples
Drata. Risk Register: How to Build One + Examples. **Drata Guide**

What is a Compliance Dashboard, And Why Do You Need One?
FloQast. What is a Compliance Dashboard, And Why Do You Need One?. **FloQast Blog**

Skills Development & Career Planning

Free Skill Development Templates
HubSpot. Skill Development Templates. **HubSpot Resource**

Free Skill Development Training Planner For 2023 Template
TheGoodocs. Skill Development Training Planner. **TheGoodocs Template**

📚 Career Clarity Map Exercise:

Write a short leadership mission statement:

List 3 short-term career goals:

List 3 short-term career goals:

🔥 Apply It Challenge:

Share your mission statement with a mentor, peer, or coach.

📈 Success Tracker:

Date	Vision Action Taken	Reflection

🚀 PART 7 of 8

📚 Section 5:

Your Cyber Leadership Commitment

📖 Concept Summary:

Leadership isn't accidental — it's a commitment you renew every day.
You are building a legacy not only for yourself but for every woman who comes after you.

You are breaking codes, breaking barriers, and building futures.

🔎 Reflection Prompts:

What leadership legacy do I want to leave in cybersecurity and GRC?

How will I lead differently starting today?

✍️ Craft Your Cyber Leadership Vision Statement:

(Write 5–6 sentences about the leader you are becoming.)

📜 Breaking the Code™ Leadership Pledge Card

- ✔ I pledge to lead with clarity, courage, and authenticity.
- ✔ I will lift as I rise.
- ✔ I will advocate for inclusion and innovation.
- ✔ I will break barriers for myself and for those who will follow.
- ✔ I choose to lead boldly, act strategically, and inspire change.

Signature: ______________________________

Date: ______________________________

📈 Leadership Milestones Tracker:

Milestone	Date Achieved	Reflection

🎯 Design Your Cyber Dream Career

📚 Vision Exercise:

✨ Imagine your ideal cybersecurity or GRC career.
✨ Dream boldly, dream freely, dream authentically.

🔎 Career Vision Prompts:

What is my ideal cybersecurity/GRC role?

What skills do I want to master?

What industries excite me the most?

What certifications or credentials will help me grow?

Where do I want to work — remote, hybrid, global companies, startups?

What salary or impact goals do I have for 3, 5, and 10 years?

✨ Your Cyber Career Dream Board

(Draw, sketch, or list anything here: companies you admire, skills you want to build, the leader you are becoming!)

✅ **END OF PART 7**

🔗 Mini Networking Strategy Plan

Building Meaningful Relationships in Cybersecurity and GRC

📖 Concept Summary:

In cybersecurity and GRC, your network is one of your most powerful tools.
But it's not just about adding connections — it's about building authentic relationships.

Relationships create opportunities.
Relationships build your leadership brand.

🔎 Reflection Prompts:

Name 3 cybersecurity or GRC professionals I would like to build a relationship with:

Professional Name	Why Connect?	First Step I'll Take

🔗 Mini Networking Strategy Plan

✍️ Networking Questions to Build Relationships:

What inspired you to pursue cybersecurity or GRC?

What has been your biggest career lesson so far?

How do you stay sharp in this fast-changing industry?

🔥 Apply It Challenge:

Reach out to **one** new person this month to start building an authentic connection.

SECTION 6:
Interview & Promotion Prep

!? Sample Behavioral Questions

For each question, reflect on a time you demonstrated these skills or qualities.

Describe a time when you identified a significant risk in a project.

What steps did you take to assess and mitigate it?

What was the outcome?

Tell me about a situation where you had to influence stakeholders to adopt a new policy.

How did you prepare your case?

How did you handle pushback?

SECTION 6:
Interview & Promotion Prep

Give an example of a project where you had to collaborate across teams or departments.

How did you build trust and ensure clear communication?

What challenges arose, and how did you resolve them?

Share a moment when you had to make a difficult ethical decision.

What factors did you consider?

How did you communicate your recommendation?

Recall a time you dealt with imposter syndrome or self-doubt.

What triggered those feelings?

How did you overcome them and move forward?

Sample Technical Questions for GRC Roles

Use these to test your foundational knowledge and prepare concise, confident answers.

What frameworks (e.g., ISO 27001, NIST CSF) have you implemented, and how did you adapt them to your organization's needs?

Your response:

Describe the steps of a risk assessment process you've conducted.

Your response:

How do you stay current on changing regulations and compliance requirements?

Your response:

Explain how you would design and track key risk indicators (KRIs) for a cyber risk program.

Your response:

Walk me through your approach to incident response and post-incident reporting.

Your response:

STAR Reflection Exercise

A STAR story uses four steps, Situation, Task, Action, Result to answer behavioral questions clearly and concisely. Briefly set the context (Situation), define your role (Task), explain what you did (Action), and share the outcome (Result). It breaks your response into four clear parts:

SITUATION: Set the scene. What was the context or challenge?

TASK: Explain your responsibility. What goal were you trying to achieve?

ACTION: Describe exactly what you did. Which skills, tools, or processes did you use?

RESULT: Share the outcome. What impact did your actions have, and what did you learn?

Step	Guiding Questions	Your Story
SITUATION	What was the context or challenge? Who was involved?	
TASK	What goal or responsibility did you have in this situation?	
ACTION	What specific steps did you take? What skills did you leverage?	
RESULT	What was the outcome? How did your actions create value or learnings?	

STAR Reflection Exercise

💥Tip: Practice telling your STAR stories out loud in under two minutes each. That clarity and brevity will impress any interviewer.

Use this same structure for any example, whether it's influencing stakeholders, handling an incident, or overcoming bias in the workplace. Practicing a few STAR stories will help you answer any "Tell me about a time when…" question with confidence and impact.

Keep this page handy as you prepare for interviews and promotion conversations. Review your STAR stories weekly, refine your technical answers, and enter each discussion with confidence, because you've crafted your own success narrative.

📅 12-Month Reflection and Celebration Pages

✨ Every month, leadership happens not just in huge wins but in small consistent steps.
Each month, reflect, celebrate, and recalibrate.

🗓️ [Monthly Pages — Same for Each Month]

📅 [Month Name]

✨ Motivational Quote:

"Your crown has been bought and paid for. Put it on your head and wear it."

— Maya Angelou

🔎 Monthly Reflection Prompts:

What was my biggest win this month?

What new skill or certification did I explore?

What professional connection did I make or strengthen?

What leadership action did I take?

What moment of gratitude do I want to honor?

📚 [Repeat this page format for January through December, each with a unique empowering quote!]

January Monthly Reflection and Celebration

What was my biggest win this month?	Leadership Action I Took
What new skill or certification did I explore?	Moment of Gratitude I Want to Honor
What professional connection did I make or strengthen?	Tip: Celebrate even the small steps —every win counts!

1 MONTH

12-Month Reflections & Celebrations.

February Monthly Reflection and Celebration

What was my biggest win this month?	Leadership Action I Took
What new skill or certification did I explore?	Moment of Gratitude I Want to Honor
What professional connection did I make or strengthen?	Tip: Celebrate even the small steps —every win counts!

2 MONTHS

March Monthly Reflection and Celebration

What was my biggest win this month?	Leadership Action I Took
What new skill or certification did I explore?	Moment of Gratitude I Want to Honor
What professional connection did I make or strengthen?	Tip: Celebrate even the small steps—every win counts!

12-Month Reflections & Celebrations.

April Monthly Reflection and Celebration

What was my biggest win this month?	Leadership Action I Took
What new skill or certification did I explore?	Moment of Gratitude I Want to Honor
What professional connection did I make or strengthen?	Tip: Celebrate even the small steps —every win counts!

May Monthly Reflection and Celebration

What was my biggest win this month?	Leadership Action I Took
What new skill or certification did I explore?	Moment of Gratitude I Want to Honor
What professional connection did I make or strengthen?	Tip: Celebrate even the small steps —every win counts!

12-Month Reflections & Celebrations.

June Monthly Reflection and Celebration

What was my biggest win this month?	Leadership Action I Took
What new skill or certification did I explore?	Moment of Gratitude I Want to Honor
What professional connection did I make or strengthen?	Tip: Celebrate even the small steps—every win counts!

6 MONTHS

July Monthly Reflection and Celebration

What was my biggest win this month?	Leadership Action I Took
What new skill or certification did I explore?	Moment of Gratitude I Want to Honor
What professional connection did I make or strengthen?	Tip: Celebrate even the small steps—every win counts!

12-Month Reflections & Celebrations.

August Monthly Reflection and Celebration

What was my biggest win this month?	Leadership Action I Took
What new skill or certification did I explore?	Moment of Gratitude I Want to Honor
What professional connection did I make or strengthen?	Tip: Celebrate even the small steps —every win counts!

September Monthly Reflection and Celebration

What was my biggest win this month?	Leadership Action I Took
What new skill or certification did I explore?	Moment of Gratitude I Want to Honor
What professional connection did I make or strengthen?	Tip: Celebrate even the small steps —every win counts!

October Monthly Reflection and Celebration

What was my biggest win this month?	Leadership Action I Took
What new skill or certification did I explore?	Moment of Gratitude I Want to Honor
What professional connection did I make or strengthen?	Tip: Celebrate even the small steps —every win counts!

10 MONTHS

November Monthly Reflection and Celebration

What was my biggest win this month?	Leadership Action I Took
What new skill or certification did I explore?	Moment of Gratitude I Want to Honor
What professional connection did I make or strengthen?	Tip: Celebrate even the small steps —every win counts!

December Monthly Reflection and Celebration

What was my biggest win this month?	Leadership Action I Took
What new skill or certification did I explore?	Moment of Gratitude I Want to Honor
What professional connection did I make or strengthen?	Tip: Celebrate even the small steps—every win counts!

Congratulations!

🎯 Closing Message:

✨ Cut out or post these affirmations where you will see them daily!

You are no longer waiting for permission.
You are no longer questioning your worth.

You are shaping the future of cybersecurity and GRC through your leadership, your authenticity, and your resilience.
Your voice, your vision, and your power are needed now more than ever

Congratulations—this is just the beginning.

✨ Final Empowerment Message

You are no longer waiting for a seat at the table. You are building new tables, new rooms, and new futures.

Keep rising. Keep breaking the code.

— Dr. Cheryl Cooper

www.ingramcontent.com/pod-product-compliance
Lightning Source LLC
LaVergne TN
LVHW071346210926
848486LV00003B/238
* 9 7 9 8 3 4 8 4 6 3 0 7 6 *